OWLS of the NORTH

A Naturalist's Handbook

Stone Ridge Press
2515 Garthus Road
Wrenshall, MN 55797
www.StoneRidgePress.com
sparkystensaas@hotmail.com

BIRD NERD NATURAL HISTORY
OWLS OF THE NORTH: A NATURALIST'S HANDBOOK

Printed in Canada by Friesens
10 9 8 7 6 5 4 3 2 1   First Edition

Graphic Designer: Mark Sparky Stensaas
Maps by Matt Kania (www.MapHero.com)

ISBN-13: 978-0-9760313-4-5   softcover
ISBN-10: 0-9760313-4-5   softcover

OWLS of the NORTH

A Naturalist's Handbook

by David Benson

Stone Ridge Press

This book is for my owling sons…

Jonas Peter Benson

and

Lars Kristofer Benson

Table of Contents

Acknowledgments

Thanks to Kim Eckert, who took me owling for the first time and even took me owling again after that. When that guy shot at us, do you think it was a warning, or was he just a bad shot?

Special thanks to the publisher, Mark "Sparky" Stensaas, who has been a great friend and conversationalist about owls and many other topics since I first came up north. Thanks to Jim Lind and John Ellis for editorial comments.

Thanks to all of my owling compatriots; these people have all been part of my lifelong owl conversation, most during the past 19 years; all of them have talked with me about owls, and some actually went out in the woods after dark with me: Jonas Benson, Lars Benson, Pam Benson, Bernie Blakeley, Dave Cooper, Kim Eckert, Paul Egeland, Jesse Ellis, John Ellis, Paul Englund, Dave Evans, Molly Evans, Jan Green, John Green, Dave Grosshuesch, Suzanne Gucciardo, John Heid, Mike Hendrickson, Ken Hoffman, Molly Hoffman, Retta James-Gasser, Bob Janssen, Don Kienholz, Bill Lane, Jim Lind, Sue McDonnell, Frank Nicoletti, Tom Shaffer, Mark "Sparky" Stensaas, Paul Sundberg, Peder Svingen, Doug Swanson, Suzanne Swanson, Bill Tefft, Larry Weber, Mark White, Terry Wiens and, last and least (but only in an alphabetical way), Steve Wilson.

I have poured as much as I can of my own experience into this book, but as with any such book, what one person can add to the body of knowledge is a small thing. My experience stands on a broad platform of the writing and experience of others. Here in the age of books, one can have a conversation with Sibley, Kaufman, Eckert, Duncan, Nero, the Suttons and all the rest. I have also spent a large amount of time talking about owls with the people named in the acknowledgments, and with many others. It's a good thing—after all, you can't go owling all the time! Well, actually, you can, but just consider what that did to . . . (y'all know who you are.)

David R. Benson
Duluth, Minnesota
September 2007

About this Book

This is a book for people who love owls. In my experience, that includes most people, who are attracted to the mystery of creatures that are active mainly at night and are difficult to see. Or maybe we're attracted to owls because of their eerie sounds. The word "owl" is an old one, and it is believed to come from an imitation of the sounds owls make.

Actually, I think we love owls for one simple reason: they are upright, vertically-oriented, short-necked, big-headed, two-legged creatures with both eyes and a down-turned beak on the front of the face, just like us!

I have tried to make the information in the book accurate and up-to-date enough to be not too annoying to experts, the book really is for anyone who is intrigued by owls, expert or not.

The other part of this book's title is "Owls of the North," and this is mainly true, but in a complicated sort of way, as is the case with all directional references. "North" depends on where you are standing. To someone in northern Canada, some of these birds are southern species. Also, I have only dealt with the northern owls of eastern North America. I'm afraid there's nothing here about Spotted Owls, Flammulated Owls, Western Screech-Owls or Northern Pygmy-Owls, all western species that could claim the title, " . . of the North" but all of them owls with which, alas, I have no experience. (I suppose we could have titled the book in eighteenth-century style: "*Owls of the North: Being a Compendium of Trivia and Wisdom About The Diverfe Owls of the Northern Reaches, Including Most of the Owls of North America, but Not Those owls of the West Coast of the United States and Southern Canada . . .*") Further, Burrowing Owls

and Barn Owls, which do occur in the Southeast, are not addressed. Nevertheless, this book works for all of the "northeastern half" of North America, and for much of the rest as well.

It has been my pleasure to talk about owls, listen to owls and look for owls with hundreds of people at Hawk Ridge, in state parks, on the Superior Hiking Trail, at the birding festivals in Grand Marais, Minnesota and in many other places. To the countless people who've come with me on trips when we missed the bird, "The contents of this book are what you can see if you stick with it!" To those of you who did get to see the bird, "Gloating is unseemly." I hope all this owl information isn't, as they say in Greek, "like carrying owls to Athens," i.e. too much of a good thing.

In Jane Yolen's fine "children's book," *Owl Moon*, the story of a father and daughter who go owling together, the daughter says, "My brothers all said sometimes there's an owl and sometimes there isn't." Truer words were never spoken. This can be frustrating for those of us who are used to the quick gratification of watching nature programs on television, where every few seconds, we get a satisfying look at a fascinating phenomenon of the wild.

So while you wait for the excitement of seeing or hearing an owl, let that frustration spur you to notice the ordinary fruits of owling: the chance to experience a spring night in the woods: the smell of melting snow and balsam poplar sap, a landscape lit by northern lights or a full moon, quiet—deep quiet, and all the connections of a new world—the real world.

Short-eared Owl *Asio flammeus*

Description: An owl of open country. Often seen floating over fields with a bouncy, butterfly-like flight.
Range: Circumpolar. Found across much of Canada and the Northern Plains to Interior West.
Size: Height 15 inches, weight 12 oz.
Wingspan: 38 inches.
Other Names: marsh owl, prairie owl.
Hibou des Marais
  (French: "owl of the swamps")
Jorduggla
  (Swedish: "ground owl")
Lechuza de la Penas
  (Spanish: "quill feather owl")
Diet: Mainly voles but other small rodents including mice, shrews and gophers.

1

Short-eared Owl

The wet smell of an early summer marsh and the hum of mosquitoes set the stage for one of my favorite owl memories. I arrived at a grassy swamp in northern Aitkin County, Minnesota a while before dusk. Nothing was moving in the still air when out of the distance a bird came gliding into view. It wheeled and darted low over the marsh, skimming above the tips of the grass, then gliding up higher, dropping and coasting. In a few seconds, another Short-eared Owl joined the first, and then another and another, until there were seven, dancing above the hazy grassland. I watched for maybe twenty minutes before the dark hid the owls from my view.

Identification

Short-eared Owls are medium-sized owls with almost-invisible ear tufts. (They're there, but on most individuals, you won't see them—they are so short, and often tucked against the head.) The overall impression is of a mottled, buff-colored bird. They have spotted, dark-and-light backs, vertical streaks on the breast and dark patches around yellow eyes. Females are darker and more richly-colored than males.

Looks very much like a Long-eared Owl in flight, with a buffy patch on the outer wing, and a dark patch at the "wrist," but on Short-eared note the pale trailing edge of the wing (dark on Long-eared); also note the contrast in colors on a Short-eared: the streaks underneath extend only a short way below the head (the rest of the underparts are pale), and the rump is paler than the back. Short-eared owls have a very light wing-load (see sidebar this page), so they can fly slowly, hover and maneuver easily above their hunting grounds.

Wings & Weight

Ornithologists compare different species with a measurement called "wing-loading," which is a ratio between the weight of a bird and the surface area of its wing. Birds with high wing-loading carry a lot of weight for the size of their wings. These are birds like Great Horned Owls, which are built with a strong bone-and-muscle structure to support their weight and the weight of large (in comparison with their own bodies) prey. In general, these are forest species which spend most of their hunting time perched, watching for prey, and then strike with direct, forceful, dropping stoops.

Birds with low wing-loading, like Short-eared Owls, have a more delicate bone-and-muscle structure. They are open country birds, they have long wings and their low body weight allows them to drift, hover, back off, glide forward and search for prey as they float over field and meadow.

Sounds
Generally not heard, but makes a sharp bark like a small dog.

Habitat
Open country, especially wetlands, but also found in dunes, on tundra and in other grasslands. In winter, seen in stubble fields, coastal dunes and shrubby areas.

Range
Found across North America, this is a cosmopolitan owl which also lives in South America, in Eurasia and on some Pacific Islands, including Hawaii. Short-eared Owls migrate out of the northern part of their range in fall, and they are seen at northern hawk watch sites on occasion. In the central and southern parts of their range, they appear to stay all year. May be declining, probably due to loss of habitat.

Food
Mostly eats voles, but also many other types of small mammals including mice, shrews, rabbits, gophers, bats and muskrats. May also eat birds. They cache (store) prey to feed their young, which gives them some margin in case they fail to catch prey or the weather is bad. Owl populations fluctuate along with local populations of small rodents.

Hunting

Hunts by flying low over the ground, dropping down to catch prey. Though they have excellent vision, apparently hunts mostly by hearing. They have asymmetrical ears like the owls that hunt exclusively by hearing. Most active at dawn and dusk, but seen during the day more than most owls. In keeping with its preference for open country, Short-eared Owls can often be seen roosting in the open.

Courtship & Nesting

During courtship, the male flies up into the air in an elaborate "sky dance," gives a few short hoots, and then glides down, making some wing-claps under his body as he descends.

The nest is a shallow depression in a dry area, lined with grass and feathers. Incubation is done by the female. The male feeds the female, and then after hatching, the male brings food and the female feeds the young. She will also hover over the young in cold weather. The young can leave the nest after 12 to 18 days, and they can fly at 27 to 36 days. The adults defend a threatened nest by making wing-claps or by perching near the nest and fluffing up to look as large and aggressive as they can.

Juveniles

Tawny white; with a dark face and light eyes; a darker, vertical stripe on the middle of the forehead.

Behavior

Short-eared Owls sun-bathe, holding their wings open as they face into the sun. They also dust-bathe, which helps rid them of bugs.

Feather & Muscle

Owls have dermal (under, but near, the skin) muscles that attach to follicles, each of which holds a feather. Typically, there is a muscle that erects and a muscle that depresses each feather, and these pairs of muscles work in concert with other pairs, so that all the feathers work together smoothly.

The movement of feathers in flight is the most easily seen use of these muscles, but it is seen so commonly that it is often not recognized for the marvel that it is. Several owl species alter the position of the feathers that make up their ear tufts. This would be another commonly seen example, if the owls weren't so blamed hard to see in the first place!

Short-eared Owls will occasionally congregate in large numbers, like the small group I saw in Minnesota. This is apparently in response to a large supply of rodents. In winter, they may roost in groups, and occasionally one or more Short-eareds will roost with a group of Long-eared Owls.

1. Nestlings hunkered down in a ground nest.

2

Owls & Mice

Paul Johnsgard calculated that an average Barn Owl, who would eat about 90 grams of food per day, is likely to eat about 33 kilograms of animals, which would be almost entirely small rodents like mice, each year. If one assumes at least ten years of life for this owl, that means the owl would eat about 725 pounds of mice in its lifetime. At the weight of the average mouse, that would be 11,000 mice!

Short-eared Owls, Barn Owls, Northern Saw-whet Owls, Boreal Owls, Long-eared Owls, Northern Hawk Owls and Great Gray Owls all have diets composed of over 90 percent small mammals. The four other species in our area that are not dietary specialists, Screech-Owl, Barred Owl, Horned Owl and Snowy Owl still eat 70 to 75 percent small mammals. The only exceptional species in this area is the Burrowing Owl, whose diet is over 90 percent invertebrates (especially insects). A world without owls would be a world full of mice!

2. Conflict or courtship? Talon-clasping is a rarely witnessed behavior in Short-eared Owls.

Long-eared Owl *Asio otus*

Description: A strictly nocturnal owl of woodlands. Medium-sized with ear tufts.
Range: Circumpolar. In North America across southern Canada south to central and southwest U.S. Migrates from North in fall.
Size: Height 15 inches, weight 8 oz.
Wingspan: 36 inches.
Other Names: Wilson's owl.
Hibou Moyen-Duc
  (French: "middle duke owl")
Hornuggla
  (Swedish: "horn owl")
Búho Chico
  (Spanish: "little horned owl")
Diet: Mainly small rodents; rarely birds, bats and snakes.

I leaned out over the bridge, watching the placid, glass-like drift of the river below. The only thing in earshot was the buzzing of mosquitoes, and then, the one long note of a Long-eared Owl. I had heard them at this bridge several times and it was a pleasure to hear that call again: simple, clear, long and almost goose-bump inducing. Long-eared Owls are one of the harder owls to see—they are quite rigorously nocturnal, and they live in woodlands. Still, their long, single note is a pleasure to hear.

Identification

A medium-sized owl; quite tall in profile. True to their name, they have long ear tufts, but the tufts are often compressed against the head and hard to see. The ear tufts are close together where they meet at the head (unlike Great Horned Owls, which have a relatively broad expanse between the ear tufts). The eyes are orange-yellow. Long-eared Owls have a reddish eye-shine in artificial light.

A perched Long-eared Owl may, at first glance, look like a miniature Great Horned Owl, but along with the difference in the placement of the ear-tufts, notice the dark vertical stripe near the eyes and the dark, blotchy striping on the breast (unlike Great Horned, which has noticeable fine, horizontal barring).

Looks very much like a Short-eared Owl in flight, with a buffy patch on the outer wing, but on Long-eared note the dark trailing edge of the wing (pale on Short-eared); also note the

Ear Tufts

Some owls have ear-tufts, horn-like projections of feathers on top of the head. In spite of the popular generic image of an owl, which includes ear-tufts, most owls do not have them. Only a quarter of the 200 or so species of owls in the world have tufts. The name "ear-tufts" only refers to their place and appearance. So far as we know, they have nothing to do with hearing.

"So far as we know" is the key phrase because we really don't know why some owls have them. One theory is that they are a form of mimicry, meant to look like the ears of mammals, maybe cats. This would be more plausible if owls were out and about in daylight, when the tufts could be seen. Plus, it is unclear how this mimicry would help the owls. It seems that appearing more like another predator might scare off more prey. If the mimicry is intended to scare off predators of the owl, other objections arise, including that owls of some sizes might actually be more vulnerable if they were mistaken for a mammal.

Another theory is that the ear tufts help with camouflage — that somehow the tufts break up the profile of the owl or look like sticks so the owl is harder to see in a tree. This theory has in its favor the fact that the owls with prominent tufts do tend to be woodland owls (although there are other forest owls, like Barred Owls, who do not have tufts). Against this theory are, again, the

(Continued on page 17)

more uniform color of a Long-eared: the streaks underneath extend from the head almost to the tail, the rump is the same color as the back and the upperwing across the back is fairly uniform. Short-eared Owls give a lighter, more contrasting general impression: the rump is slightly paler than the rest of the back, and the streaks underneath only extend a short way below the head (the rest of the underbody is pale).

Sounds
Most characteristic call is a long, single hoot—longer than the hoots of Great Horned or other owls. Also makes a surprising variety of other sounds, including barking (like a small dog) and squeaking. You may have heard one and had no idea it was an owl.

Habitat
Prefers woodlands with some open country for hunting—a forest bird, but a bird of the forest edge. Roosts in dense conifers in winter. On the prairie they take advantage of the mature arborvitae or red cedar groves that have grown up around parks or cemeteries.

Range
Found across North America, from the tree line south into Mexico. Lives year-round in some areas, but clearly migrates out of some northern areas, as evidenced by large movements observed at Hawk Ridge

in Duluth and other northern migration-watch sites. Also found across Eurasia.

Food

Eats whatever small rodents are plentiful in its area, but has been recorded consuming a variety of small creatures, including birds, snakes and bats.

Courtship & Nesting

In courtship, the male displays by flying around the nesting area with glides and wing-claps. The nest is usually in a tree at least four feet off the ground. Does not build nests but uses nests abandoned by other birds such as hawks, ravens or crows. The female incubates the eggs for 26 to 28 days. The male feeds the female on the nest. The female stays with the young for the first couple of weeks after hatching. Young can move out of the nest after three weeks and can fly after five weeks. The male will continue to feed the young until they are at least ten weeks old.

Juveniles

Pale gray (when nestlings) or rusty-tan with pale horizontal barring; "bumps" on the head where the ear tufts will be; dark patches around light eyes and a gray bill.

1. This juvenile has assumed its defense posture. Spread wings make the youngster appear larger to predators (see sidebar on page 21).

Ear Tufts
(continued)

fact that owls spend much of their time in the dark, when the tufts cannot be seen; and the placement of the tufts, which varies from species to species and would hardly function in the same way if this were there primary purpose. It might be a secondary purpose, however. Owls with small ear-tufts that are barely visible, like Short-eared Owls or Snowy Owls, clearly are not using them for camouflage, but apparently they serve some purpose even for these open country birds.

Finally, Karel Voous describes the case of a tame Long-eared Owl, who allowed himself to be petted and scratched about the head; but if the ear-tufts were touched, immediately the owl taloned the toucher hard enough to draw blood. Maybe ear tufts are some kind of perceptive organ, or maybe they relate to emotional expression. Nobody knows.

Behavior

All members of a Long-eared Owl family—male, female and young—play a role in territorial defense. The complex vocalizations exhibited by parents and their offspring change during the breeding season. This unusual territorial defense system evidently ensures great hunting and breeding success, which has specialized food habits and is limited to hunting at night.

Long-eared Owls favor communal roosts in the winter. It is not unusual for a roost to contain 30 to 50 owls, and sometimes there are over 100. This means that if you find signs of one Long-eared, you should keep looking. Clumps of conifers in cemeteries are good places to check, as are dense conifers anywhere near open country. Long-eareds often roost low in the tree—maybe only three or four feet off the ground.

Owl Vision

Owls have their eyes on the fronts of their heads like humans do, which gives them good binocular vision; but unlike humans, they cannot rotate their eyes around in the sockets, so to get a different angle on something they're looking at they bob and move their heads around.

Young owls often go through a developmental phase of bobbing and shifting their heads, as they learn how to use their keen eyesight and hearing (photo below). Adults will also shift or bob their heads to get different angles on something they're looking at.

Owls have spectacular low-light vision. Their eyes are packed with receptors, and their vision at night is between ten times and a thousand times better than ours. The trade-off for all those receptors is a poor sense of color. Owls see perfectly well in daylight, but they don't see much color.

Great Horned Owl *Bubo virginianus*

Description: Widespread large owl with ear tufts. Found in many habitats from boreal forest to prairie to mountains to desert.

Range: All over North America and south through Mexico. Only absent from the open tundra where nesting sites are nonexistent.

Size: Height 22 inches, weight over 3 lbs.

Wingspan: 44 inches.

Other Names: big cat owl, hoot owl.

Grand-duc d'Amérique
  (French: "grand duke of America")

Buho Cornudo
  (Spanish: "horned owl")

Diet: Wide variety of prey from mice up to porcupines. Also rabbits, skunks, snakes, fish, birds and even other hawks and owls.

This owl is the one you're most likely to see or hear. How can I say that when I don't know where you are? Because this is one of the most widely-distributed birds in North America. They live in the Far North; they live in the Deep South. They live near the tundra; they live in the desert. They live in cities; they live in wilderness. They live everywhere in between.

Many times, coming home from a long day in the field, I have chanced upon the blocky profile of a Great Horned Owl atop a spindly-looking tree at dusk. There is something shocking about this—you've got that tired, aired-out feeling, and it feels as if all you've seen for hours is trees, and then, this big owl out in the open. Great Horned Owls are aggressive and powerful hunters. They often hunt from a high perch (another reason you could see one) and swoop down on prey far below. One of their nicknames is "tiger owl," which does give an impression of their ferocity in the hunt.

Identification

This is a big, bulky owl with ear tufts. Its eye has a yellow iris, and it has a white patch on the throat. This patch is indistinct in shape, unlike the "bow-tie" of a Great Gray Owl. Many Great Horned Owls have orange facial disks, but some are gray. The undersides show a fine, dense, horizontal barring. The overall color of the feathers ranges from brownish to grayish, and even to frosty-white in birds of the Far North (see sidebar on page 25).

The most likely species to be confused with Horned Owls are Long-eared Owls. Reading a descriptive text (like this one!)

Defense Posture

When threatened, owls will follow one of the common-sense facts of the natural world— "bigger is more dangerous." That is, they'll puff out their feathers, lift their wings to increase both their height and breadth, and maybe throw in a few hisses for good measure; these acts are all intended to convince the threatening party that it is not dealing with a mere "hoot-owl;" no, this is a large, indeterminate foe, and if you know what's good for you, back off.

Adults and juveniles (pictured below) will both use this tactic in times of duress. This young Great Horned Owl obviously thought the big bad photographer was a real threat.

might give you the idea that Long-eareds look like miniature Great Horned Owls: distinct ear-tufts, brown over-all color with a rusty-colored facial disk. The general impression that each owl gives, though, is quite different—Horned Owls are big, stocky birds; Long-eareds are smaller, thinner birds. If you're not sure, look at the bases of the ear tufts. The ear-tufts of Great Horned Owls are spaced relatively far apart, leaving a broad top-of-the-head between. The tufts of Long-eared Owls are relatively close together, and if the tufts are erect, they are much longer than those of other owls. In addition, Long-eareds have more black on the face, and their undersides lack the fine, horizontal barring of a Horned Owl. Barred Owls, which in our area are found throughout much of the range of Horned Owls, lack ear-tufts, have dark eyes and have a completely pale bill. They also have a ring of horizontal barring around the neck.

Great Grays appear as large as Great Horned Owls, but they lack ear-tufts, and they have a distinct, white, bow-tie mark at the front of the throat. The breast of a Great Gray is more blotchy-appearing, with less distinct barring. Great Horned Owls usually do appear more brown than Great Grays, but this is not always the case. Snowy Owls are really only similar in size, but the pale, northern form of Great Horned can be just as pale as a Snowy. Note the ear-tufts and the gray face of a pale Great Horned Owl; Snowy Owls lack ear tufts and have white faces in all plumages.

Great Horned Owls have a red eye-shine in artificial light.

Sounds

The most common call of a Great Horned Owl is a clear hooting—something like the sound that many people think all owls make. If you are close enough to hear it clearly, it comes in patterns of five: medium-short-long-long-long. Sometimes I remember it by "*I'm a GREAT HORNED OWL*." with great emphasis placed on the words in the name.

Another typical sound, not heard so often, but distinctive when it is heard, is the sound of nestlings. Even while still in the nest, these are big birds, and their high-pitched "*Oink!*" is a puzzling sound when encountered in the woods.

Great Horned Owls can also make many other sounds. I once tracked down what I thought was a cat in a tree, only to find that it was a Horned Owl.

Habitat

Found in almost every habitat, but may avoid open country like tundra or grassland during the breeding season.

Range

Found across the United States and Canada north to the tree line and south throughout Central and South America. They are found in a wide range of habitats from prairie to deciduous forest to desert to mountains, and they are common birds. There is no regular migration but individuals may wander a long ways in fall and winter.

Mobbing

When birds find a predator, they will sometimes mob the bird. This involves flying at the intruder, making a racket and sometimes a direct attack. Owls are frequent targets of mobbing, especially by crows.

Mobbing can take different forms. I watched a flock of Pine Grosbeaks array themselves in a tree around a Hawk Owl and flick their wings and tails — no noises, no attacks, just flicking. Often, as in this case, the owl seems oblivious to the attention. However, I once saw a Great Horned Owl being chased by crows. The crows made strikes at it; and then, just like that, the owl swung its feet upward, grabbed a crow, killed it with one squeeze, dropped it and continued on its way. The owl pictured below has also nabbed a crow.

One idea of why birds mob is the "move along" theory: raptors (hawks get mobbed too) rely so much on surprise that, if the surprise can be removed, they lose their advantage and aren't so dangerous.

Food

Great Horned Owls are renowned for eating a wide variety of prey. Their diet is on average about 75 percent mammals, ranging in size from mice up to rabbits, skunks and even porcupines. They will also eat birds up to the size of geese, lizards, snakes, insects, scorpions and fish. This species is considered a potential predator of almost every bird species in North America, including hawks and other owls.

Hunting

Great Horned Owls hunt from a perch, often from the tip of a tall tree. They hunt mainly at night, but sometimes at dusk or dawn. In winter they are sometimes out during the day, though not with the frequency of some other owls. In areas with few tall trees they will use rocky ledges or buildings as hunting perches.

From their perch, they use their excellent hearing and low-light vision to spot prey, swooping down from above to make a kill with their exceptionally large and powerful talons. (This is one of the most difficult birds for banders and other scientists to deal with in the hand.) Their aggressiveness, power and size sometimes lead them into trouble. There are records of Horned Owls dying as they tried to kill a porcupine.

Courtship & Nesting

Because they nest during late winter in the North, they can take advantage of the cold to help store their food. They will catch and kill prey and then leave it to freeze near the nest. When they need the prey for food, they will incubate it, just like an egg, until it thaws and is edible again.

Great Horned Owls are usually the first birds to begin nesting after the new year. There are records of nesting in January, and many are on the nest in February. Young Horned Owls are big birds and their bodies take time to develop. The early nesting year probably helps give them enough time to learn how to hunt before the next winter closes in.

Most Great Horned Owl nests are large bowls of sticks—the former nest of some other large bird, such as a hawk, crow or heron. True to their variable habitats, however, Horned Owls will also nest on rock ledges, in caves, in the tops of broken-off tree stumps or even on the ground. They do very little to prepare the nest. Sometimes they will partially line the nest with feathers.

Males do a simple courtship display flight, and they feed the female as a courting behavior. Usually there are two or three eggs in the nest, but there can be as many as six. The female does most of the incubating, which takes 28 to 35 days. Both parents hunt for the young owls, which get big and hungry quite quickly; they can leave the nest by climbing as early as five weeks after they hatch, which is about five weeks before they are able to fly. The family group stays together for several

'Arctic' or 'Taiga' Great Horned Owl

A form of the Great Horned Owl, known as the "Arctic" or "Taiga" Great Horned Owl, is much frostier in background color than the owls seen throughout much of the continent. These birds are seen mainly well to the north, but some winters they may show up as far south as the northern tier of states.

"Taiga" (pronounced *TIE-guh*) is an evergreen landscape form of the north. Taiga Great Horned Owls are aptly named. They are not albinos, or even partial-albinos; rather, like many northern creatures, they have a paler cast than their southern relatives.

months and the parents continue to do most of the hunting and feeding during this time. Mates stay together until one of the pair dies.

Juveniles
Color is variable as with adults; fairly distinct horizontal barring, lighter head feathers create a "helmet"; light eyes and a dark bill.

Behavior
In the northern part of their range, the population cycles of Great Horned Owls seem to follow the Snowshoe Hare cycle because these hares make up a large part of their food in the north. Every ten years

---

1. A foolhardy Gray Squirrel checks out its neighbors. The nestlings are curious but do not yet recognize it as prey.

the number of Snowshoe Hares grows and then declines. This phenomenon is driven by the interplay of the food supply and the lives of the hares. When food becomes more abundant, the hares have more babies. Then the next year, there are more parents who have more babies; and so on in succeeding years, until the population of hares gets to the point where the food supply isn't enough to sustain them through the long, cold winter. Then some hares die from starvation, and the ones who survive have fewer babies the following year. Horned Owls follow in the wake of this cycle. After the increase has begun, it becomes easier for them to find food (hares), and the population grows: more Horned Owls survive, and the ones that survive have more babies in response to the availability of food. When the hare population drops, fewer owls survive the winter, and the survivors have fewer babies the next year. In reality, the situation is more complicated—Horned Owls eat many other animals too; but the fact that this pattern can even be detected shows how important Snowshoe Hares are to Great Horned Owls.

Owls Who Eat Owls

Since they are carnivores, owls sometimes eat other owls. As the biggest and strongest, the Great Horned owl is most likely to do the eating; there are records of them eating Barred Owls, Eastern Screech-Owls, Long-eared Owls, Short-eared Owls, Barn Owls, Burrowing Owls and Saw-whet Owls; and one could guess that they have eaten others too, including perhaps other Great Horned Owls.

Snowy Owls have been recorded eating Short-eared Owls and Saw-whet Owls (and Gyrfalcons!) Barred Owls have been recorded eating Long-eared Owls and Screech-Owls. (There is also one record of a Barred Owl and Northern Goshawk both dying when one tried to eat the other — I'll bet it was the Goshawk who started it.) Northern Hawk Owls have eaten Boreal Owls. Great Gray Owls have eaten Northern Hawk Owls.

In most, if not all, owl species, at some point in the development of the nestlings, the larger, stronger young eat the smaller, weaker young. This provides even more nourishment for the thriving young, and it removes the weaker ones from using the food supply. Brutal as it is, it enhances the success of that particular brood.

One owl's partner is another owl's meat!

Barred Owl *Strix varia*

Description: Nocturnal owl of mature deciduous forests and swampy woods. More often heard than seen. Large without ear tufts.

Range: Eastern North America south to Gulf Coast and west across southern Canada to Pacific Northwest and southeast Alaska.

Size: Height 21 inches, weight 1.6 lbs.

Wingspan: 42 inches.

Other Names: woods owl, swamp owl.

Chouette Rayée
  (French: "hoot owl")

Buho Listado
  (Spanish: "striped owl")

Diet: Mainly small mammals, but also birds, crayfish, salamanders, frogs and insects.

One of my favorite owl experiences was staying at a camp set on a flat hill surrounded on three sides by river valleys in southern Wisconsin. As dusk settled, Barred Owls began calling. At least four individuals called back and forth. Their rich, distinctive calls continued all through the evening, giving us a deep sense of being enveloped by the wild.

On a number of other occasions my encounters with Barred Owls have been silent ones—on a walk in the woods, something caught my peripheral vision, and I looked up to see a perched Barred Owl, looking at me steadily, making not a sound.

Identification

The Barred Owl is a large-to-medium-sized owl without ear tufts. Its name comes from the distinct, vertical, dark barring against a light background on its chest and belly. It also has horizontal barring in a band around the neck. Unlike most owls, its eyes are dark. If you see this owl in a light at night, watch for a strong red eye-shine. The face is somewhat heart-shaped, but it's a broad, squat shaped "heart."

Sounds

If you hear a Barred Owl in full call at close range, you'll never forget it. The rich, strident klaxon, often described as sounding like, "*Who-cooks-for-you?-Who-cooks for you'all?*" mainly rises through the first two phrases and then slides down the scale on "*you'all.*" At a distance (and the call can carry over long distances), you might not hear the complete pattern and

Why all the Noise?

Even though much of their vocalizing goes on when we don't hear it, owls are very vocal creatures. In the late winter and spring, the males of all owl species call their distinctive calls, hoping to attract a female, or to signal to their paired female that breeding season is upon them, or to denote that they are in an occupied territory — other owls need not apply. In some species, the females join in, echoing or dueting with the call of the male.

Once the eggs have hatched, new sounds enter the picture — begging calls, yelps, squeaks and a myriad of other sounds. When the birds have fledged, the young specialize in a simple, frequent call which serves to tell the adults where to bring the food. Later in the summer and into fall, family groups of some species (notably Barred Owls) will chorus together in a way that can make the listener feel surrounded.

Of course, there are a bunch of other sounds too — bill-clacking, wing-clapping, hissing, rattling and others that are used for courtship, to warn intruders, for emotional expression (probably) and for reasons we have yet to figure out.

you might have to strain a bit to tell if you're hearing a dog or an owl.

Barred Owls will often sing in duet or even in chorus. Song researcher Donald Kroodsma has shown that females sing with a higher-pitch and more tremolo in the "*y'all*" portion of the song. You might be able to tell who is who if you hear a duet. In late summer, family groups will call back-and-forth to each other—one of the aural highlights of the outdoors.

Like almost all owls, Barred Owls can make a variety of sounds, and you may need to see the owl to tell which kind is making the sound (or if it's even an owl that you're hearing!)

Habitat
Prefers woodlands, especially wet woodlands like river bottoms and wooded swamps. In the North, it can be found in coniferous forests, but throughout much of its range seems to prefer deciduous or mixed woodland. Like its close cousin of the West, the Spotted Owl, the Barred Owl likes to live in deep woods. Since they tend to stay in the same woods for years, their familiarity with the area helps them hunt even in the deepest darkness.

1. This composite photo shows a Barred Owl approaching, catching and carrying off a rodent in complete darkness.

Range
Found throughout the eastern United States as far west as the Great Plains and well north into southern Canada. Its range also extends west through part of Canada and then south into the northern Rockies. Barred Owls are quite sedentary—no mass migrations for them.

Food
Eats mostly small mammals, but will also eat birds, frogs, salamanders, snakes, crayfish and insects. The wide range of food in the diet fits for a bird that lives across such a broad expanse of the continent, and which is found in quite varied habitats, including wet ones.

Hunting
Less aggressive than the Great Horned Owl (the other largish woodland owl in our area), Barred Owls also seem to be less likely to perch in the open. They will, however, hunt during both day and night, especially at dawn and dusk. In winter, a Barred Owl seen hunting during broad daylight may be the harbinger of tough times for owls and an incursion of northern owls of several species into more southerly areas.

Hunts mostly from perches, but will hunt on the fly in search of prey, and will hover briefly before stooping on prey.

Courtship & Nesting
Courting includes male and female bowing, bobbing, raising their wings and calling while perched close together. Nests in large tree cavities or in old nests of hawks or crows.

Albino Barred Owl?

Not exactly. The bird in these pictures is leucistic (pronounced loo-SIS-tik), that is, the cells which ordinarily produce colors are somehow not working. Albino birds lack these cells altogether. Leucistic birds usually appear merely paler than normal plumage birds, while albino birds usually appear completely white; but often it is difficult to tell. The bird in these pictures has brown eyes, so it is not a true albino. True albinos are exceedingly rare. [This bird was photographed in Duluth, Minnesota in 2005.]

Juveniles
Pale brown with blotchy, wide barring; dark face with indistinct rings around eyes, dark eyes, yellow bill.

Behavior
Barred Owl is sympatric with Red-shouldered Hawk. Their ranges are quite similar (though Red-shouldered Hawks aren't found west of the eastern Great Plains); and their preferred habitats are identical. Because one raptor is nocturnal (the owl) and the other diurnal or daytime (the hawk), these two species can coexist without excessive competition. They will even use the same nest (though not in the same year!).

Pellets, Whitewash and Skulls

Owls usually swallow their prey whole. An owl catches a mouse, kills it with its talons or by biting its neck and then bolts the whole thing down. Much of the mouse is not very digestible though — the bones, fur and other tough parts don't provide much nutrition. These are compacted together in the owl's digestive tract. Then, about six hours after the meal, a pellet of these indigestible parts is coughed up and it drops to the ground beneath where the owl is roosting. Owls generally produce two pellets a day, so if you find a pile of twelve pellets, odds are the owl has been roosting there for six days. Pellets last for a while — maybe even a whole season — but eventually the rain and the weather wear them down. All that's left then is the biggest, thickest part of the prey's body — the skull. So, a little pile of rodent skulls can also be a sign that an owl has been present.

The size of owl pellets matches the size of the owl. The small owls have pellets the size of the end of your smallest finger. Medium-sized owls have medium-sized pellets. Great Horned Owl pellets are long and thick. Hawks also eject pellets, but hawks tend to strip the meat off their food before they swallow it, so their pellets contain few bones, and they don't hold together as well as owl pellets — you're not so likely to find them in the woods.

Another sign of owls in the woods is whitewash. If you see whitewash in the branches of a tree or on the ground beneath the tree, it may be the sign of an owl. Owl whitewash is thick and waxy, not unlike dried pine sap. The owl just drops it beneath itself. This is in contrast to hawks, who have similar whitewash but spray it out away from the tree, so it covers a larger area, farther from the roost tree.

Owls are so well camouflaged that these signs will often be the best way to detect their presence.

Great Gray Owl *Strix nebulosa*

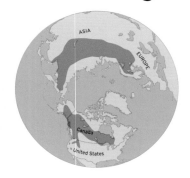

Description: Tallest owl in North America, and one of the most elusive. A bird of the boreal forests of the Far North.

Range: Circumpolar. In North America breeds from Alaska to Yosemite, Rocky Mountains to Minnesota. Large irruptions south in some winters.

Size: Height 27 inches, weight 2.5 lbs.

Wingspan: 52 inches.

Other Names: spruce owl, cinereous owl, sooty owl, spectral owl.

Chouette Lapone (French: "Lapland owl")

Lappuggla (Swedish: "Lapland owl")

Cárabo Lapon (Spanish: "Lapland owl")

Diet: Almost exclusively voles but may take rabbits and other small game in times of starvation.

Big snowflakes drifted out of a gray sky, and the wind that had chapped my face all day finally subsided, and then I saw my first Great Gray Owl. It was perched atop a spindly aspen tree, about twelve feet off the ground, at the edge of an opening in the forest. I got out of my car and set up my scope to watch. The owl paid me no attention; it just continued to scan the ground in front of it.

The main impression I had was that it seemed so odd for such a big bird to be on such a little tree, and that the tree should have been bent way to the ground by such a big bird. Most of the size is feathers and not muscle and bone, but there is something dramatic about seeing the broad wings and large-looking body of one of these birds.

I was able to approach quite closely without seeming to disturb this owl. Most likely it was some combination of intense hunger and perhaps lack of experience with humans that led this bird to ignore me. This is not uncommon with birds that come south in the winter; local birds tend to be much more wary.

Identification
Large gray owl with no ear tufts. The face is flat, which, with the rounded back of the head, gives a distinctive profile. It has a fairly plain, gray back. The underparts show blotchy, vertical barring. The facial disk has dark, concentric rings, like the annual rings of a tree. The eyes are yellow and the bill is pale. A good field-mark is the bright white "bow-tie" mark

Functional Feathers

Our species of owls have wings that are well-adapted for hunting at night in perfect silence: the leading edge of the wing is serrated, the trailing edge is fringed and the upper surface is downy and soft. This feather arrangement makes almost no sound as the owl flaps through the air, allowing for maximum surprise. Fish Owls, which do not live in North America, have wings that make lots of noise when they flap — their prey, living beneath rushing water, is not scared off by the noise.

Preening, as this Great Gray is doing, keeps all feathers aligned, silent and in good condition. Owls also coat their feathers with an oil that is secreted from the uropygial gland at the base of their tails. This oil gives the feathers a protective coating.

underneath the bill. This can be seen even in poor light and can help you distinguish this owl from Great Horned Owls (large, but with ear tufts and only an indistinct white patch under the bill) and Barred Owls (not so large, lacking ear tufts and lacking any distinct white beneath the bill).

In flight, note the large size, the large "squared-off" head; long, broad wings; lighter panels near the ends of the wings, and indistinct, dark bar at the end of a long (for an owl) tail.

Most differences between Great Grays seen in the field will simply be differences between individuals. However, you might be able to tell the relative age of some birds. First year birds will have uniform gray flight feathers with pale tips. Each succeeding year, they will molt some, but not all, of these feathers; so that after the first year, their flight feathers will be a mix of young and old feathers, which will give a mot-tled look to the wing. Look especially at the tips of the primaries, which will be plain and dark on adults. Look also at the tips of the tail feathers, which will be pointed on young birds and rounded on older birds. For many birds, it will not be easy to tell.

Great Grays are more likely to be albinistic (white) than other owl species, but it is still rare (see *Dark Gray and Light Gray* sidebar on page 45).

Sounds
The call is a deep, muffled series of hoots descending slightly in pitch. The tone quality is much less clear than the hoots of a Horned Owl. The female has a distinctive nest call, a rising "*Whoop!*"

Habitat
Great Gray Owls choose areas that feature both dense forest for roosting and open country for hunting. They like bogs, which may have dense tamarack

The Great Invasion of 2004-2005

Periodically, large numbers of northern owls move south into Southern Canada and the northern tier of the United States during fall and winter. The most noticeable of these invasions (movements of owls outside of their range) or irruptions (movements of owls in large numbers into new areas that are, nonetheless, part of their range) involve Great Gray Owls. In recent decades in Minnesota, there have been big Great Gray Owl years beginning in the autumns of 1965, 1968, 1977, 1983, 1988, 1990, 1991, 1995, 1996, 2000, 2001 and 2004. You can see that the intervals are irregular.

None of these irruptions/invasions can compare, however, with the winter of 2004-2005. From mid-November to mid-April, 5,225 Great Gray Owls were reported in Minnesota; the prior record was 494 owls in 2000-2001. There were Great Grays everywhere in Northeastern Minnesota; Warren Nelson saw 51 in 45 minutes in Aitkin County; another group saw over 200 Great Grays in one day!

People who never pay attention to birds saw the owls. They were in the news, in conversation and in the dreams of lots of people that winter. Not only were there lots of Great Grays, but there were over 475 Northern Hawk Owls and 600 Boreal Owls reported. Exceptional numbers of northern owls were seen across much of southern Canada, from Québec through Ontario and across the prairie provinces. Three birds made it to Iowa, and scattered birds were seen well south of their usual territory.

Unfortunately, some of the birds who come south in a year like this die. Some are found starved, and a distressing number are hit by cars. The medians and shoulders of highways are prime rodent habitat, and the owls end up standing on the road or flying low on the hunt. Many of them, hungry if not starving, are so focused on their prey that they don't see the cars speeding down upon them until it's too late.

Beyond saying that there is a relationship between lack of food and the movement of the owls, not much is known for sure. In the months preceding the invasion, there were low populations of the rodents these owls eat, and biologists such as James Duncan in Manitoba saw that there was little owl breeding during the summer of 2004. As with Snowy Owl invasions, there are multiple cycles at work. Intensive work by biologists who banded, determined the sex of and measured owls during 2004-2005 gave much more detailed information than had been known before about the structure of the invasion and the characteristics of the birds who came. Some of their research overturned older ideas, such as that invasions were composed mostly of young birds. Still, data from different places revealed different patterns — yet another indication that the situation is far more complex than we might have imagined. There is a lot that we simply don't know.

We do know, however, that these invasions present us "southerners" with some of the most spectacular wildlife-viewing ever.

stands adjacent to open wetland. In many parts of their range, they prefer to nest in tamarack bogs.

Range

Great Gray Owls are truly northern birds, ranging across Eurasia and from Alaska across northern Canada to Quebec; some also live in the northern Rocky Mountains and Sierra Nevadas. In general, they are considered to be non-migratory, but they are famous for their winter invasions of more southerly areas. During these incursions, they have been seen well into the Midwest, and they have at times been common sights in certain areas; notably, around the city of Winnipeg, and in the Sax-Zim Bog area north of Duluth, Minnesota.

Food

In keeping with its smaller-than-it-appears size and

1. Locals in Finland (the country, not the town in Minnesota) put out baskets for the owls to nest in; and surprisingly, several did.

relatively small feet and talons, it mostly eats small rodents (mainly Meadow Voles and Red-backed Voles), but will take larger prey on occasion. During a recent incursion of these owls into Minnesota, Great Grays were seen taking prey as large as Snowshoe Hares. This was in extreme circumstances, however, and Great Grays ordinarily eat only rodents and occasionally birds.

Hunting

Great Grays hunt from a perch. Their light weight means that they can sometimes be seen perched atop very spindly trees. When they hear prey, they glide down for the kill. Their acute sense of hearing allows them to hunt for prey even beneath the

2. An adult delivers prey to its mate at the nest. The rodent will likely go to their hungry nestlings.

A Field Guide to Voles

Voles are a staple to the Great Gray Owl. The top two are their main prey species.

Meadow Vole *(Microtus pennsylvanicus)*

Gapper's Red-backed Vole *(Clethrionomys gapperi)*

Prairie Vole *(Microtus ochrogaster)*

snow, sometimes several feet below the surface. They can break through a snow-crust thick enough to hold the weight of an average man.

Courtship & Nesting

During courtship, the male will feed the female. Also during courtship and at other times, Great Gray Owls will preen each other, a behavior that is believed to reduce aggression and signal safety. They nest in old stick nests of other species, such as Northern Goshawk or Common Raven; they will also nest at the top of a broken-off conifer and rarely on the ground. A pair may reuse the same nest for several years. The female incubates the eggs for 28 to 36 days. The male feeds the female on the nest. Once the young are hatched, the female continues to brood them for another two to three weeks. The male continues to bring food, which the female feeds to the young. The young are able to climb out of the nest after three to

Owls' Ears

Their ears are on the sides of their relatively broad heads, far enough apart so that they can gain good directional hearing along a horizontal axis. This is like human hearing. If you were to stand in an open field and hear a noise in front of you, you could judge quite well from which direction the noise was coming.

Unlike humans, most owls also have asymmetrical ears; that is, the opening on one side of the head is higher in the skull than the ear on the other side of the head. This fact wasn't recorded until 1870 and the first scientists who noticed it thought that it was an anomaly of the individual owls on which they saw it, a birth defect or something like that. By 1881 though, it had been confirmed that lots of owls had asymmetrical ears.

It would be as if one of your ears were upside down. This gives owls good hearing along the vertical axis. Humans can pinpoint direction, but are not very good at judging precisely how far away the sound is. Owls can pinpoint the direction left to right, and the direction up and down. This is critically important for them, because it means that in sheer darkness, they can swoop to a precise location in front of them, rather than just heading in the right direction and then flailing around trying to find their prey.

In addition to asymmetry, owls have facial disks, which help funnel sound to their ears, and many owls have flaps near their ears which they can move to help make their hearing even more acute.

four weeks and can fly one or two weeks later. In at least some instances, the female leaves after the young fledge, and the male continues to feed the young for as long as three months.

Juveniles
Medium-pale gray with faint horizontal barring; pale bars on the wings; dark patches around eyes; light eyes and pale bill.

Behavior
Great Grays are believed to have two sleep periods each day. They are active at dawn and dusk, but sleep at midnight and midday. Their small yellow eyes probably work best in the daylight. At night their eyes dilate until they are wide-open and would appear dark, if you could see them.

They avoid hot weather and roost in densely-shaded trees during the middle of the day in summer. When roosting, they lower their head, close their eyes and

Deep Snow Hunting Technique

In this sequence of photos, a Great Gray comes in for the kill. Having left a perch where it heard its prey under a foot and a half of snow, the owl glides in with wings expanded and tail flared as to stabilize and regulate speed. When the location of the prey is reached, the owl stalls out and hovers momentarily before tipping quickly forward and diving into the snow face first.

The Great Gray's feet are tucked under the chin to help break any crust and to be ready to grab the prey. Snow tunnels that the vole had created collapse and they are temporarily trapped by the mini avalanche. The Great Gray's long legs and sharp talons sift through the snow grasping for the prey (bottom photo). Successful or not, the owl then checks for danger and lifts away, leaving a distinctive "plunge hole" in the snow.

This deep snow hunting ability allows Great Grays to inhabit northern forests in winter that other avian predators must seasonally abandon.

"fold" the facial disk in a way that leaves a vertical line on the face that helps blend in with bark patterns.

Great Gray Owls are often not skittish around humans. During summer, they are hard to see, but during winter, especially when northern owls come south, they can sometimes be approached without being agitated. In some cases, this is because they

are intently hunting; it may just as well be because they are lethargic from hunger (Note that the if the owl appears agitated, you should back off immediately. You should also never approach an owl near a busy roadway, lest your presence cause the owl to fly to its death on the highway.) Several observers have noted cases of Great Grays seeming to follow them out of curiosity. I once stood with a group, peering into a dusky tamarack bog where we had heard a nest cry. After several moments of silent watching, one of my students tapped me on the shoulder and pointed at the Great Gray that had flown in to an open perch about fifteen feet behind us and sat quietly watching us watching the bog.

Dark Gray & Light Gray

Not all Great Grays are gray. Plumages can vary from very dark (like the bird photographed near Superior, Wisconsin) to very pale (like "Linda," a bird in Finland named after a famous blond violinist). Albino and melanistic birds are quite rare.

Snowy Owl *Nyctea scandiaca*

Description: Large white owl of open country. Also found in industrial areas in winter.

Range: Circumpolar. In North America only nests on the open tundra of the continent's northern fringe. Some move south to northern and central U.S. each winter.

Size: Height 23 inches, weight 4 lbs.

Wingspan: 52 inches.

Other Names: Arctic owl, great white owl.

Harfang des Neiges
  (French: "owl of the snows")

Fjälluggla
  (Swedish: "mountain owl")

Diet: Lemmings on nesting grounds but in winter will eat ducks, rabbits, hares, pheasants, rats and carrion.

One winter day, on a lunchtime walk, I heard a group of crows making a racket. When I found them, they were circling a frosty white male Snowy Owl perched on the edge of an office building. They didn't get too close, but they were able to make the Snowy move from building to building. The flock of noisy, black crows, and the stark white owl made quite a scene as they moved around above the heads of the oblivious people who walked and drove on the streets below.

This white ghost of an owl is seen only in winter across most of our area; a time when its white and black feathers provide good camouflage against the backdrop of snow.

Identification
The dominant impression of a Snowy Owl will be of a big white owl, although some have extensive dark bars on the top of the head, the back and the flanks. The face will always be white. They are small headed, and their smooth plumage gives them a compact look. Some of the pale northern "Taiga" Great Horned Owls will be as light-colored as a dark Snowy Owl, but note the Horned Owl's ear-tufts and gray face. These two owls aren't especially likely to be seen in the same habitat, but I have seen Snowy Owls on the corners of buildings, for example, and Horned Owls perched on ice or the ground.

A white-morph or pale gray-morph Gyrfalcon might look superficially like a Snowy Owl; but note the Gyrfalcon's long tail, somewhat pointier wings and yellow feet, along with at least some dark smudges on the face. Gyrfalcons are very rare

Snowy Owls & Airports

Because Snowy Owls have such a strong preference for open country, they are drawn to airports, fields, industrial areas and frozen lakes when they come south in the winter. On frozen lakes they can be very difficult to see since they look just like a clump of ice. Sometimes, it's a matter of waiting for an ice clump to move to tell whether or not it's an owl.

At northerly airports like Vancouver and Toronto, there have been collisions between planes and Snowy Owls. To prevent this, some owls have been banded and relocated. Another creative solution has been to have a falconer send a large raptor down the runway ahead of the plane. The owls see the eagle and fly off, and the airplane can take off safely.

in most of our area, but, like Snowy Owls, they are seen in winter, they will hunt in the near-dark and they frequent open areas. The handful of winters when there's been a Gyrfalcon around Duluth, where I live, there have usually been Snowy Owls in the vicinity. In good light, you wouldn't be likely to confuse the two, but given only a quick look in twilight, you might.

It is possible to speculate or even tell their sex and age of Snowy Owls based on how much dark feathering is present against the white background. For example, a bird with extensive dark barring will most likely be a young female; a bird that is almost pure white will be an older male. Some young males and older females will be hard to discern, but pay special attention to the extent of the white bib (larger on males) and to the tail—males usually have no more than three dark bars across the top of the tail and females usually have at least three dark bars.

Snowy Owls are unique in several respects. Their bodies are more completely covered with feathers than any other species—the bill is almost hidden, the feet are almost covered and beneath the toes are hair-like fibers that are longer and more extensive than those of other birds. Snowy Owls actually do have ear tufts, but they are not visible under usual circumstances.

1. Winter may bring some Snowys south. Preferred locations seem to be open areas with abundant prey; often industrial areas in urban settings.

Note that any owl can seem very light-colored in the beam of a flashlight or headlight.

Sounds
Silent most of the year and unlikely to be heard except on the high breeding grounds where the male will make deep hooting sounds.

Habitat
Open country, including tundra, grassland, marshes, beaches and dunes. Breeds on Arctic tundra from just north of the tree line to as far north as possible.

Range
Across northern Alaska and Canada (and around the globe in the North). In summer found only in the Far North, beyond the tree line. In winter, many birds move south to Southern Canada or the Northern U.S. Seen every year in southern Canada, the Dakotas, Montana, Minnesota and New England; seen most years in the Maritime Provinces, Pacific Northwest, the Midwest and the Mid-atlantic states; seen occasionally in the southern Great Plains and in Northern California.

Food
Prefers small mammals, especially lemmings, but in winter will eat a wide variety of prey, including hares, squirrels, ducks, fish and carrion. One killed and ate a Great Blue Heron at Logan Airport in Boston.

Linked to Lemmings

The migration of Snowy Owls is not well-understood. They apparently move to follow prey in summer, and while the general idea that they come south in winter when lemming populations crash is no doubt true, it isn't the entire truth. Lemmings have different population dynamics in different areas, and the two species of lemming that make up much of the Snowy Owl's diet have different cycles. Add to this the Snowy Owl's own fluctuations in breeding and the picture is more complicated yet. Over the past century, the average interval between invasions to the south is around four years, but this is an average and the size of the invasion can vary greatly.

The lifecycle of Snowy Owls also correlates strongly with the population cycles of two species of lemming — the Brown Lemming (*Lemmus trimucronatus*) and the Peary Land Collared Lemming (*Dicrostonyx groenlandicus*). An adult may eat up to 1600 lemmings in a year. A large proportion of the population of Snowy Owls times its breeding to coincide with the four-year peak cycle of the Brown Lemming. When the lemmings are plentiful, almost all adult Snowy Owls breed and may lay up to twelve eggs. Then very few of them breed at all until the top of the cycle comes again four years later.

2

Hunting
Snowy Owls may hunt from a perch (although given the owls' preference for open country, the perch may be no more than a grassy hummock or a chunk of ice). If the perch is high enough, Snowy Owls prefer to approach from below and glide up to the perch, rather than dropping down to it from above.

Courtship & Nesting
When courting, the male flies with deep, slow wing

2. Nests on the tundra are placed directly on the ground. Predators are often lured away with a broken wing act.

beats, sometimes carrying a lemming in his bill, lands near the female and bends forward in a pose not unlike that of a grouse, with wings spread and tail pointing up. Snowy Owls, which move around a lot during the course of a year, mate with a different partner each year.

On the nesting grounds, Snowy Owls defend their nest, which is right out in the open, by first adopting menacing postures, and then by flying and carrying out a bluff routine to draw predators away. In this display, they fly a short distance then fall to the ground and then get up and run, struggling along as if they have a broken wing and squawking and squeaking. Karel Voous reports that one intruder was led over two miles away from a nest in this way. We don't get to see such antics here in the south, where most sightings are of roosting owls that are notably inert.

Juveniles

Uniform gray with a white face, yellow eyes and a dark bill; only seen in the Far North.

Behavior

Snowy Owls are one of the few species of owl that has been seen swimming—at least it's been seen in water, paddling with its wings for a short distance.

Life in the High Arctic

Since some Snowy Owls stay in the High Arctic all winter, they survive some of the coldest, wintriest conditions of any animal on earth. Only one other kind of bird, the Adelie Penguin, has better insulation from its feathers, and the feathers of a Snowy Owl insulate as well as the best-insulated arctic mammal fur, that of the Arctic Fox and the Dall Sheep. They also have unusually thick layers of fat beneath their skin. It is still something of a mystery what they do for food in such conditions, since there are few animals present. However, they can spend long periods of time conserving energy by not moving, and they can survive long stretches (as much as a month!) without eating.

Northern Hawk Owl *Surnia ulula*

Description: A medium-sized day-hunting owl with a long tail. A bird of the Far North.
Range: Circumpolar. In North America ranges across the continent from Alaska to Quebec and south to Minnesota. Irruptions south in some winters.
Size: Height 16 inches, weight 11 oz.
Wingspan: 22 to 28 inches.
Other Names: day owl, Hudsonian owl.
Chouette Eperviere
  (French: "sparrowhawk-owl")
Hökuggla
  (Swedish: "hawk-owl").
Diet: Primarily voles and mice. Occasionally will take larger slow-moving birds like grouse.

Rare birds are supposed to be hard to find. If they were easy to spot, they wouldn't be rare; which is why I couldn't believe my eyes the first time I saw a Northern Hawk Owl. I was a beginning birder, and when I arrived at the location where someone had seen a Hawk Owl, I didn't really expect the bird to be there. I certainly didn't expect the bird to be there in midday, which was the only time I could go; and I definitely did not expect the bird to be perched in the top of a nearby black spruce, bobbing its tail and looking down at me imperiously.

Yet, that's how it was for the first, and for all of the other Hawk Owls I've seen. The Northern Hawk Owl is an exception to many "rules" about owls, and the biggest exception is that it is diurnal (that is, it hunts during the day as a matter of course). One of the old names for this species is the "Day Owl" (they will also hunt in the dark). No need to get up at 0-dawn-hundred to find this owl. Sleep in and head out whenever you're ready. Wait until winter is well underway, since outside of a relatively small number of nesting records, Hawk Owls are only seen in the winter in Southern Canada or the U.S.

Because they are a bird of the Far North, many people never get to see one of these birds, but if a Hawk Owl is in the area, you won't be likely to miss it. They spend the day perched atop a tree or post, and they will often hunt from the same perch, or at least the same area, all winter long. In Duluth a few years ago, one Northern Hawk Owl earned the nickname, "The Kohl's Owl," because it parked for the winter in a spruce grove

How can an Owl be like a Hawk?

In evolutionary theory, the similarities between the Northern Hawk Owl and a hawk is an example of convergence. The idea is that, even though these species are not closely related genetically, the environments in which they live have shaped their development in similar ways. Just as living in the ocean has left whales (mammals) and fish with many common characteristics, living in the North Woods has left Northern Hawk Owls and true hawks with much in common as well.

near the Kohl's store.

Hawk Owl is a good name for this bird too, since in habit and appearance, the Hawk Owl falls between the hawks and the other owls. Their long tail and manner of perching make them look like a hawk; and their rapid wing strokes and hunting dive from a high perch are also hawk-like. Hawks also hunt during the day.

Identification

"A blob with a long tail" —Hawk Owls are often seen first from a distance, perched on the top of a tree, so that their distinctive silhouette is the only feature that can be seen; and though it's possible to see other owls during the daytime, Hawk Owl is the most likely species to be seen then, within its range. They are medium-sized owls, gray-brown in color (sometimes very gray, sometimes quite brown).

1

With a closer look at a perched bird, you can make out the yellow eyes, the black frame on a pale face, the fine, brown-and-white barring on the underside and the long tail. From the side, the frame on the

1. The silhouette of a Hawk Owl in the tip-top of a tree is unmistakable; truly a blob with a long tail.

face looks like a bold black stripe. The back is a mottled gray-brown and the nape of the neck has dark marks that, with a little imagination, suggest the face of an owl. Maybe this helps dissuade Northern Goshawks or other large predators from taking a shot from behind. Hawk Owls have a dark "mustache mark" underneath the bill. The whole facial pattern seems to give the bird a fierce expression.

In flight, a Hawk Owl is like a Cooper's Hawk; they are about the same size, both have a maneuverable flight and the flight profile can be surprisingly similar. Watch for the facial stripe and the more-pointed wings of a Hawk Owl. The flight might also remind you of a falcon, with fast, direct wing beats . A Hawk Owl can look like a big, fat Merlin in flight.

It's unlikely you'll confuse a Northern Hawk Owl with anything else, but Boreal Owls also have black facial frames, and Northern Shrikes, which are much smaller and quite different in most ways, do perch atop spruce trees in winter and bob their tails.

The age of Northern Hawk Owls can be determined if you get a good enough look at the tail. First year birds have a chevron-shaped white area on the end of the tail (The shape is due to the pointed, white tips of their tail feathers.) Older-than-first-year birds have a crescent-shaped white area at the end of the tail (The tips of their tail feathers are rounded.)

Sounds

Because so few Hawk Owls nest far enough south to be near

Swivel Vision

Can owls swivel their heads all the way around? Nope, but they can swivel them about 270°, which is so far that it can seem as if they went all the way around. This ability helps greatly when searching for prey from a perch.

many people, you may not ever hear this species. If you are lucky enough to be near a potential nest site during breeding season though, you might hear the loud, ringing, repetitive call, often described as "*ul-ul-ul-ul-ul-ul,*" etc. These calls can last up to 30 seconds and be repeated frequently. Both males and females will make this call, sometimes as a duet.

Around an actual nest, you might hear a wide variety of yelps, hisses and bill snaps—sounds that are quite similar to the nest sounds of other owls. When nesting adults feel threatened, they will make a sharp "*kwit kwit*" or "*ki-ki-ki*" sound.

The only Hawk Owl sound that I have heard outside of the breeding season is a soft "*tweep tweep tweep*" sound from birds that were perched and actively hunting.

Habitat

Hawk Owls prefer open areas with hunting perches such as open spruce forest, tamarack bog and burns or blowdowns. They like the same types of landscape for nesting. During winter irruptions/invasions, they often hunt near roadsides or on farmland with trees, buildings, telephone poles and electric wires.

Range

Hawk Owls breed in the boreal forest across North America (and for that matter, across Northern Europe and Asia). Usually Hawk Owls remain in the Far North all winter, but in some years they move southward, appearing as far south as the northern tier of states in the U.S. They are one of the few species of birds whose range is almost entirely north of the U.S./Canada border. Northern Minnesota and the Upper Peninsula of Michigan are the only spots in the lower 48 states that see Hawk Owls with any regularity.

In Northern Minnesota, invasions/irruptions of Northern Hawk Owls generally occur in the same years that other northern owls (Great Gray, Boreal and Snowy) are more common. While these years often spell disaster for Great Grays and Boreal Owls, Northern Hawk Owls seem to do better, probably because they eat a more varied diet and can switch prey preferences if necessary. In 1996-1997, when 263 Boreal Owls were seen in Minnesota, 202 of them were found dead or dying. During the same winter, 100 Hawk Owls were seen, and only one was found dead. Hawk Owls are also less likely than the other species to hunt low along the shoulders of roads, so fewer are hit by cars.

Occasionally following an invasion year, a pair will attempt to nest south of the Canadian border. However, there are few nesting records, and these owls are likely to nest in remote areas, so it is difficult to tell if there really are more nests after an invasion winter.

Staying Warm

The northern owls, who spend much of their lives in the cold, need ways to keep warm. One of these strategies involves holding their body feathers erect to trap more air around their bodies and hold in more warmth. The Hawk Owl below has done this, giving it a less-sleek appearance than it usually presents.

The technical term for this feather fluffing is piloerection. Tiny muscles under the skin contract and tug at the base of individual feathers when the bird is cold. Not only utilized by birds, piloerection also causes mammal fur to fluff and is actually what we humans call "goose bumps."

2

Food

Hawk Owls eat small rodents, like voles and mice. In the winter they are known to eat grouse and ptarmigan, large slower ground-feeding birds that frequent the same landscape. There are also records of Hawk Owls eating a wide variety of other birds and small mammals, and even medium-sized mammals like Snowshoe Hares, but small rodents are their bread-and-butter, so to speak.

Hunting

Hawk Owls hunt from a convenient perch, searching for prey by sight and then swooping quickly down for the kill. They will chase prey for short distances, and sometimes they hunt from perch to perch, dropping down for prey and then swinging up to a nearby perch if they fail to catch their target. Hawk Owls have also been seen hovering over potential prey—unusual behavior for an owl (see photo on page 56).

Alone among owls, Hawk Owls have a falcon-like notch in their bill. Falcons use the notched part of their bill to sever the spinal cords of their prey. Owl species often use their bills in a similar way, and presumably the notch helps the Hawk Owl to do this with more efficiency.

2. Wing prints in the snow mark the spot of a Northern Hawk Owl hunting foray.

Congruent with their daytime activity, Hawk Owls rely on sight more than hearing for hunting. Their ears are symmetrical, so they apparently do not need the kind of precision hearing used by most other owls. When scanning for prey, Hawk Owls lean forward almost to the horizontal and pump their tails (a most "un-owly" posture). When they strike, their drop off the perch can look almost like an accidental fall until they begin to glide to the kill.

Courtship & Nesting

Hawk Owls nest in cavities in decayed trees, open hollows where the tops of trees have broken off, or vacant woodpecker nests. Hawk Owls do not build nests in these holes; they simply use them as they find them. In the tops of hollow trees, the incubating bird is left open to all kinds of weather. In all kinds of nests, the owl's long tail can sometimes be seen sticking out of the nest.

The breeding season usually begins in February. During nesting, the female does all the incubating, and the male does all the hunting. Hawk Owls are aggressive defenders of their nests and will do damage to human scalps that approach the nest. The only known predators of adults are Great Horned Owls, Great Gray Owls and Northern Goshawks. Perhaps because they don't encounter humans very much, Northern Hawk Owls are quite tolerant of our presence (away from a nest, that is). Paradoxically, some researchers have reported simply lifting the female off the nest and setting her nearby while they inspect eggs or band nestlings, and then replacing her when they are

Food Hoarding

Catching prey is not easy. I have seen hundreds of raptors come close to catching prey, but I have only seen them succeed a few times. In spite of their physical advantages, most raptors must rely heavily on surprise to catch their food.

But when the hunting is good, Northern Hawk Owls, Great Horned Owls, Saw-whets and Boreal Owls will catch extra prey and then cache (hide or store) it — as the Hawk Owl is doing in the photo below. When the prey is frozen, as is often the case for Horned Owls, the owls "incubate" it by sitting on it before it thaws. Caching allows the owls to spread out their food supply and cover times of scarcity.

done—all without drawing attack. I'm not sure anyone knows how to tell which owls will attack; the life of an owl-bander is one big gamble.

Juveniles

Mottled gray back; pale head feathers create a "helmet;" yellow eyes and bill; dark face; gray-brown, indistinct barring on underparts.

3

Behavior

Hawk Owls are a pleasure to watch. Which other owls perch in broad daylight and sit still so you can look at them through a spotting scope?

3. Four chicks snuggled into the deepest nest cavity ever recorded in North America: 23.75 inches deep. Note the size difference of the chicks.

State
Wildlife
Management
Area

open
to public hunting

Minnesota Department of Natural Resources

Owl Feet

Owls have four talons at the end of four toes. The outer toe can be pivoted back and forth to help grasp squirming or slippery prey. The only hawk who shares this trait is the Osprey, which eats fish.

Owls generally use their talons to grasp and kill their prey. In the larger owls, the talons are sharp and powerful (Ask a bird bander what it's like to handle a Great Horned Owl.) The smaller owls have smaller feet, but the talons are still sharp and lethal.

In the 1970s, Carl Marti measured the force necessary to open the clenched talons of several species of owl, finding that it only required 500g to force Burrowing Owls to open, 1,350g to force Long-eared Owls to open and a whopping 13,000g to force Great Horned Owls to open.

Northern Saw-whet Owl *Aegolius acadicus*

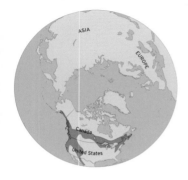

Description: Small owl of coniferous forests. Nocturnal and rarely seen.
Range: Treeline in Canada south to Great Lakes, New England, Pacific Coast south to Mexico. Yearly mass migrations south.
Size: Height, 8 inches, weight 3 oz.
Wingspan: 17 inches.
Other Names: Acadian owl, white-fronted owl, Queen Charlotte owl.
Petite Nyctale
  (French: "little night-owl")
Lechuza Cabezona
  (Spanish: "big-headed owl")
Tecolotito Cabezon
  (Spanish: "big-headed little owl")
Diet: Mice, voles and small birds.

One of our smallest owls, Northern Saw-whets can be tough to see, perched close to the trunk of a thickly-branched conifer. Their call can be hard to detect too, though paradoxically, it is fairly loud and distinctive! The first view of a Saw-whet Owl almost always elicits "*oohs*" and "*aahs*"—they are undeniably cute. I like Saw-whet Owls, although I don't think I could go so far as one writer, who wrote that the species "has beauty, talent, character, curiosity and personality."

Once, standing in a parking lot along the Gunflint Trail in Minnesota along the Canadian border, I had a little duet going with a Saw-whet. As it came closer, it seemed to raise its song in pitch, and I noticed it was speeding up a bit at the end of the phrase; so I responded in kind. The owl moved closer and closer, each time raising the pitch and accelerating at the end of the pattern. I'm not sure what it said to me on the last phrase, sung from about ten feet away, but I know now that it wasn't friendly, because at the end of the last phrase the owl flew right at my head, brushing wings and talons over my cap (Thank God for caps!) as it struck. I guess I allowed my excitement at dueting with an owl to lead me over the line into annoying the owl.

Identification

This is a very small owl, with a brownish tint to the feathers. It has a streaked forehead and a pale face with a darker bill. In our area, it is most likely to be confused with a Boreal Owl. Boreals are somewhat larger, they have spots instead of streaks on the forehead, and they have black frame marks on

Saw-whet vs. Boreal

Species that occupy the same niche in an ecosystem are of particular interest to ecologists; it usually means that there is something going on that they don't understand.

Boreal Owls and Saw-whet Owls have ranges that overlap extensively. They are around the same size, and they both eat lots of small rodents. But there are a few differences that apparently keep them from competing too much with each other. Boreal Owls prefer voles of the genera *Microtus* and *Cethrionomys*; Saw-whets prefer the smaller mice of the genus *Peromyscus* and shrews of the genus *Sorex*. In addition, Saw-whets prefer forests with more deciduous components, brushier undergrowth and lower perches than Boreals. Apparently, Saw-whets will react to recordings of Boreal Owl calls, but Boreals ignore Saw-whet calls, which may indicate that Boreals exert some dominance when the two species are together.

the face, as well as a relatively lighter-colored bill. Young Saw-whets are chocolate-brown, with a broad X-pattern in white on the face, centered on the bill. Saw-whets nest in cavities, which are often dark, and the X is thought to help the parents feed the young when they come in with prey—X marks the spot!

Male Saw-whets weigh no more than an American Robin, and females are only 25 percent heavier than a robin. They have a light wing-load, which allows for more maneuverability. This is not an owl you are likely to see in flight, given their preference for dark woodlands and the cover of night. Their flight over longer distances, though, is bounding, like a woodpecker's, and in the woods, reminiscent of the flight of a woodcock, dodging between the trees.

Sounds
The main call is a rhythmic, repetitive tooting—one whistled note, over and over, sometimes for a surprisingly long time. The owl got its name from one of its sounds, which reminded early naturalists of the sound of a whetstone sharpening a saw. When I have identified the whistling call for people, more than

one of them has said, "That's an owl?" or "Oh, I've heard that before, I just didn't realize it was an owl." Its monotony has a way of blending into the soundscape so that when you become conscious of it, you realize it has already been singing for some time.

This is one of the easiest owls to mimic, simply by whistling one note over and over at roughly the same pitch and speed as the owl. Sometimes an owl will whistle back at you and then move closer.

Habitat
A forest bird, it is most often found in conifers, but given this preference it nests in a variety of habitats. It is not so closely linked to conifers as the Boreal Owl. In winter it likes dense groves of trees, although this is one of the owls that will turn up at bird feeders—not to eat bird seed, but to hunt for mice that come out at night to eat seeds under the feeder. Owls at feeders are almost always under great stress, but they afford one of the easiest occasions to see these owls.

Range
Found across much of Canada and the United States, from the tree line south through the Midwest. On the Pacific Coast and in the Rockies, ranges much farther south. Saw-whets migrate in large numbers past Great Lakes banding stations in the fall. There is some evidence that they may spend the winter in the forests of the southeastern United States.

Roosting and Resting

Owls need time to rest; they do this by roosting quietly in an inconspicuous place. Some species sleep at night and some sleep during the day. Most kinds of owls find a hidden spot in a tree where they are unlikely to be noticed, either by predators or by potential prey. Others, like Snowy Owls, find a place in the open where their plumage provides camouflage. Roosting owls may tuck their heads under their wings, like this Northern Saw-whet Owl; but most often I have chanced upon them with their heads straight up.

Food
Eats mainly small rodents, especially mice and voles; but will also eat large insects and small birds.

Hunting
A strictly nocturnal bird. Hunts from perches only, usually lower perches than the larger owls.

Courtship & Nesting
Nests in a cavity in a tree, mainly in abandoned woodpecker holes. The incubation is done almost

exclusively by the female, and the male feeds her throughout this period. The young fledge when they are about four weeks old, and then the male feeds them outside the nest for another four weeks. Some females will find another mate and nest a second time in the same year.

Juveniles
Uniform chocolate brown on back; white, inverted triangle or X on forehead; yellow eyes, dark bill, brown eyes; bright, rusty underparts.

Owl Migration

Owls have been thought to be mostly non-migratory, and some individuals of this species do stay in the North in winter; but there are large movements of these owls in the fall. In late autumn every year, the banders at Hawk Ridge Bird Observatory along the North Shore of Lake Superior, catch and band hundreds of Saw-whet Owls (see photo below). In 1995 they caught over 1400 Saw-whets. They also average about 60 Long-eared Owls each year. In addition, they have banded small numbers of six other owl species. This research project has been going on for decades, so for some species, the few records could be counted as simply random instances of owls flying into the banding nets. Clearly, though, the banders at Hawk Ridge are witnessing the regular migration of Northern Saw-whet and Long-eared Owls. Also, when an unusually large number of another owl species shows up, it means something. The 43 Boreal Owls that were banded in the fall of 2004 were a harbinger of the massive movement of northern owls into northern Minnesota the following winter.

The banding stations at Hawk Ridge and other migration sites on the Great Lakes have provided almost all the information we have about the migration of owls, not to mention many other species of birds.

Saw-whet Owls wait patiently for their turn to be banded at Hawk Ridge.

Boreal Owl *Aegolius funereus*

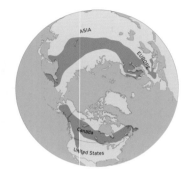

Description: A small owl of remote boreal/mixed forests in the Far North.

Range: Circumpolar. Only nests in the U.S. in Minnesota and Rocky Mountains. Irruptions south in some winters.

Size: Height 10 inches, weight 4 oz.

Wingspan: 21 inches.

Other Names: Richardson's owl, Tengmalm's owl (current name in England), funereal owl.

Nyctale Boréale
  (French: "boreal owl")

Pärluggla
  (Swedish: "pearl owl"—because of spots?)

Lechuza de Tengmalm
  (Spanish: "Tengmalm's owl")

Diet: Voles, mice and birds.

Once, near the end of a long night of conducting surveys for owls on which I hadn't heard a single owl, I stood gazing into a swampy woods waiting for the final seconds of the listening period to tick down. I admit I was a little sleepy and bored. Then, something jogged my thoughts. What was it? Was that a different sound? Now I was awake and alert. Sure enough, it was the hollow, soft, ringing call of a Boreal Owl. I smiled broadly as I checked the direction and estimated the distance from which the owl was calling. My boredom vanished as I enjoyed, for me, one of the highlights of spending time in the woods at night.

One of the most secretive and difficult to find owls, Boreal Owls are strictly nocturnal birds of the boreal forest that extends across much of central and southern Canada.

Identification
Boreal Owls are small owls with big heads (though not so small as a Saw-whet or a Screech-Owl). They are brownish-gray with spots on the back. They have black facial frames and dark markings on the face with a spotted forehead (not streaked like a Saw-whet). They have yellow eyes and a pale bill. The dark facial frames are interrupted by gray on the side of the head.

Sounds
A singing Boreal Owl makes a brief, rapid string of hollow-sounding notes: "*poo-poo-poo-poo-poo*," etc. It can sound similar to the winnowing sound made by a displaying Wilson's

Comparing the Size of Owls

We often describe owls, birds or other wildlife we see by beginning with their size, but human beings are generally not very good at judging size. Any experienced birder will have some tales of being tricked by relying on size. Size is only really useful if there is some fixed comparison one can make — with another bird or a tree that can be measured, for example. This list is by apparent size from head to tail, not by weight or wingspan.

Really Big would include the Great Gray Owl, Great Horned Owl and Snowy Owl. Medium-sized owls are the Barred Owl, Northern Hawk Owl, Long-eared Owl and Short-eared Owl. Boreal Owl would be considered small, along with Northern Saw-whet Owl and Eastern Screech-Owl. (after Johnsgard, 1988)

Snipe, another species sometimes found in similar habitat. The snipe's sound, though, is made by air passing through its feathers in flight, so the sound moves across the sky. The Boreal Owl's vocalizing is made by a perched male, so it doesn't move. In addition, the snipe's sound trails off, fading at the end; the Boreal Owl's ends more abruptly. Sounds around the nest include brief chattering and high-pitched chirping. Recently fledged birds that I have heard emit single "*beeps*" as dusk falls, as if to let the parents know where they were.

Habitat

Boreal Owls use a variety of habitat types. Singing males and nest sites are often found in mature, upland forests of mixed conifer and hardwood species. For foraging and roosting, though, they seem to prefer low, wet conifer forests.

Range

Boreal Owls live in the near Arctic around the entire globe. In North America, they nest all across central Canada. In the U.S., nests have been found in Northeastern Minnesota and in pockets of the mountain West, as far south as New Mexico. In winter,

1. Natural cavities or old woodpecker holes in aspen trees make good nesting sites for Boreal Owls.

Boreal Owls mostly stay within their breeding range, but some birds move south into North Dakota, Minnesota, Wisconsin and Michigan; there are also records from other eastern states including one in New York City's Central Park!

Food
Generally eats only small rodents, but also small birds and large insects, especially crickets.

Hunting
Hunts at night, moving from perch to perch in the forest, swooping down to catch prey. Its acute sense of hearing allows it to detect prey even under snow or in dense vegetation. Strictly nocturnal, they are most active in the couple of hours after midnight and the two hours before dawn.

Courtship & Nesting
In courtship the male sings at likely nest sites and the female chooses a suitable male. During courtship, the male feeds the female. Nests in a cavity in a tree, usually in an old woodpecker hole. In northern Minnesota, they often find good cavities in old aspen trees. They will also nest in a cavity in the top of a snag. In Europe, they readily use nest boxes. They usually do not re-use nest sites in successive years. The female incubates the eggs from 26 to 32 days. The male feeds the incubating female, and continues to feed the female and the young after hatching. After about three weeks, the female also begins to hunt. The young are then fed by both parents for about two more weeks.

Owls at Bird Feeders?

Most winters, I hear from somebody who has seen an owl at or near their birdfeeder, "Do owls eat sunflower seeds?" Nope, but they do eat animals who do eat sunflower seeds. Most birdfeeders attract more than just birds. The spilled seeds are easy food for mice and other small rodents; and the rodents are easy food for owls. If you have birdfeeders and snow, watch for the tracks of small mammals in the morning beneath the feeders.

2

Juveniles

Uniform chocolate brown on back; white eyebrow-marks; yellow eyes, pale bill; white, horizontal mark beneath bill; underparts indistinct. Juvenile Boreal Owls can look somewhat similar to juvenile Northern Saw-whet Owls, but note that Boreals have pale bills and indistinct underparts, and that the white marks on the face are more like thick eyebrow-marks than the big **X** of a Saw-whet.

Behavior

Boreal Owls will cache food; i.e. catch extra food and keep it in the nest cavity until they decide to eat it, or just leave it there! It gives the nest site that certain *je ne sais quoi*. Like Horned Owls and Saw-whets, if this cached prey is frozen, Boreals will incubate it until it thaws.

---

2. In Scandinavia, Boreals will readily use man-made nest boxes.

Owl Surveys: Sounds, Smells & Surprises

One of the tools that scientists use to assess the population and movements of owls is the survey. Most often this involves going out after dark to listen for owls, following a protocol (a specific, uniform way of conducting the survey) over a standardized route. It seems like a simple idea, but there is still lively debate about the most effective way to do this. Some surveys play a recording first and then record which owls respond. Others are passive, in that no recording is played — one just listens for a set period of time. In both cases, one must decide how long to listen, how to note what is heard, how far apart the listening stops should be and other factors.

Personally, I dislike using recordings for owl surveys. I would rather just listen for my three or five or ten minutes, taking in what comes. Either way, most owl surveys produce a lot of "negative data" — stops which produce no owl calls. This can start to wear on the surveyor if the survey has many stops; it's dark, you're alone, you're tired, there are no exciting owl vocalizations to pep you up and it can get long. A frequent topic of conversations among owl surveyors is how bad their routes are. Of course, it's all data, but the subjective experience of the person doing the route is something entirely different.

All in all, though, I love running owl surveys. While conducting owl surveys, I've seen Timber Wolves, Pine Martens, Fishers, Moose, Black Bears and even a Lynx. Often the sky has been on fire with northern lights (aurora borealis). One night the aurora lit up the sky so brightly that the woodcock starting beeping again, as if it were dusk. Plus, the spring night provides so many other interesting sights, sounds and especially smells — melting snow, balsam poplar sap, blossoms, mink, fox and skunks.

I've had some other excitement on owl routes too. I've been shot at, hollered at and creeped out in various ways. I have heard strange, disturbing noises that I could not identify. Once I passed two semi-trucks parked on a remote road. Stuff was being loaded from one into the other. I didn't stop to ask.

Oh, I forgot to mention that by doing owl routes, I've had the pleasure of hearing hundreds of owls call.

Eastern Screech-Owl *Megascops asio*

Description: Small owl of deciduous forests, wooded suburbs, prairie woodlots and river bottoms.

Range: Eastern North America from southern Canada to the Gulf Coast. West to the foothills of the Rocky Mountains.

Size: Height 8.5 inches, weight 6 oz.

Wingspan: 20 inches.

Other Names: [Formerly *Otus asio*] little horned owl, little cat owl, shivering owl.

Petit-Duc Maculé
  (French: "little spotted duke")

Tecolote Chillón
  (Spanish: "shrill owl")

Diet: Small rodents and insects, but also birds, worms, frogs, bats and even fish.

Eastern Screech-Owls spend much of their summer lives in trees, but the first one I ever saw, in the winter, was in a Wood Duck house, and probably that's the way many have seen Screech-Owls. The duck houses provide the right size hole and cavity for winter roosting. I had been tipped-off about the owl in the duck house, and I didn't have to wait long when, for unknown reasons, the owl pushed its small head with ear tufts out of the hole.

This tiny owl is widespread in the eastern United States. As is the case with many bird species, this one is poorly named, since it ordinarily does not "screech," but whinnies or trills.

Eastern and Western Screech-Owls were once considered to be the same species, but they are now seen as two separate but closely-related species.

Identification
A very small owl. Screech-Owls have prominent ear-tufts, but they are often held close to the head, so it may appear that the owl doesn't have tufts. The eye has a yellow iris, and the face is framed in black. The bill is pale. The undersides are heavily streaked, especially on the upper breast. There are two color morphs of this owl, red (a bright, rusty color) and gray. In our area, most owls are gray.

There are four small species of owl in our area. Eastern Screech-Owl is the only one with ear-tufts, so unless they are flattened against the head, the ear-tufts and size would give

Gray & Red:
Color Morphs of the Screech-Owls

Eastern Screech-Owls come in tow color patterns: gray and rusty-red. Both are found across almost the entire range of the species, and about one-third are red. A small number of birds seem to be intermediate between the two. It's not entirely clear why one species has these two colors, but there are some small differences in how the colors and metabolisms of the two colors interact, so the color may be related to environmental conditions in different parts of the range.

you a clear identification. If you see a small owl with no apparent ear-tufts, things may be a bit trickier. Saw-whets do not have black-facial frames, and the barring on the chest is white and rusty-colored, not black-and-gray or black-and-rusty. Saw-whets also have distinct, though small, white streaks on the forehead and the white markings on the face are concentrated in the center, around a darker bill. Boreal Owls do have black facial frames, like Screech-Owls, but the facial disk has more extensive white outside the eyes, and they have distinct, though small, white spots on the forehead. The streaking on the breast of a Boreal Owl is an indistinct light-and-brown. Boreals are also a bit larger than the others, but this is hard to judge without direct comparison. Boreal Owls are birds of the Far North, so in most locations, it would be truly rare for them to show up within the normal range of the Eastern Screech-Owl.

Albinism has been observed in this species, but it is very rare.

Sounds
Screech-Owls call in duet at breeding sites, using both a descending, whinnying sound, and a long, slow trill. This trilling call is similar to the sounds made by toads, but it is a slower trill. Contrary to their name, they don't screech.

Habitat
Open deciduous woodlands or farm groves. Screech-Owls will settle in a variety of habitats that are mostly open but with enough large trees to provide nest cavities. They spend the day roosting in dense cover.

Range
Eastern Screech-Owls are common through most of the eastern United States, ranging from the Gulf Coast northwards into Southern Canada and west from the Atlantic all the way to the foothills of the Rocky Mountains. They are quite rare in Northern Minnesota, Northern Wisconsin and the Upper Peninsula of Michigan. Probably absent from some areas due to lack of tree cavities.

Food
Roughly two-thirds of the diet of Eastern Screech-Owls consists of small rodents, and another third is insects; but they will eat a

Find the Owl:
Cryptic Coloration

This hard-to-see Eastern Screech-Owl is hidden mainly by its cryptic (hiding) coloration. The lines of color on its feathers mimics the lines in the bark on the tree behind it. In addition, this owl has squinted its eyes almost shut, so they are hard to see, and stretched its body to look tall and skinny, so none of it sticks out beyond the profile of the tree trunk. Compare this bird to the other pictures in this section, where the owls are relaxed.

wide variety of food, including birds, beetles, moths, crickets, bats, mice, frogs, spiders and even fish.

Hunting
Screech-Owls hunt at dusk and at night. They usually hunt from a perch, swooping down after their prey. However, they will chase flying food on the wing. Sometimes they will "flycatch" from a perch, darting out from a tree into a swarm of junebugs or moths, nabbing some prey and then returning to the perch. They have excellent hearing as well as acute eyesight.

Courtship & Nesting
Mated pairs preen each other's feathers. Courtship includes bowing, wing-raising and the clicking of bills.

Screech-Owls nest in cavities in trees, such as abandoned woodpecker holes or rotted sections of tree trunk. They will readily use nest boxes. Many birders have seen their first Screech-Owl peering out of a Wood Duck nest box. The female incubates the eggs for an average of 26 days. The male brings her food during this time. Both parents feed the hatched young. Screech-Owls stay with the same mate from year-to-year.

Juveniles
White at first; then brown-gray on back; gray on underparts, with indistinct, horizontal barring; dark eyebrow-marks; pale bill.

Behavior

Screech-Owls have been observed bringing Blind Snakes (a worm-like creature) to the nest. The snakes burrow into debris in the bottom of the cavity, feeding on insects there and possibly helping protect the young from insect infestations.

1. This adult was picking earthworms off a sidewalk and bringing them to the nest.

2 & 3. A juvenile downs a Yellow Warbler in one gulp.

Sympatry

Sympatry is when two species, similar in some way, occupy and thrive in the same area when one might think there would be too much competition between them. Owls and corresponding species of hawks are the classic examples of sympatry. Eastern Screech-Owls and American Kestrels, small falcons, are sympatric. They share much of the same range, eat much of the same prey, nest in the same type of cavity and prefer the same type of open habitat with trees. How do they do this without constantly competing for food and other resources? Easy — the kestrel takes the day shift and the screech-owl takes the night shift.

There are several other examples of sympatry between hawks and owls: Great Horned Owls and Red-tailed Hawks, Barred Owls and Red-shouldered Hawks, Short-eared Owls and Northern Harriers. Short-eared Owls and Harriers, not closely related genetically, share the same coursing hunting style, a similar long-winged, lilting flight and a facial disk of feathers that aid hearing. Barred Owls and Red-shouldered Hawks will often alternate using the same nest in alternate years — but never in the same year!

Despite the superficial similarities, owls are not especially closely-related to the hawks. Characteristics that separate owls from hawks include that owls do not have crops for digesting their food, they have their eyes on the fronts of their heads rather than on the sides, they have an outer toe that can be rotated to the back of the foot and they usually have asymmetrical ear openings.

Bibliography

Alcorn, Gordon Dee. 1986. *Owls: An Introduction for the Amateur Naturalist*. Prentice Hall. New York, NY.

Baicich, Paul, and Colin J. O. Harrison. 1997. *A Guide to the Nests, Eggs and Nestlings of North American Birds—2nd Edition*. Academic Press. San Diego, CA.

Benson, David R. 1999. *Companion of the North Winds: Northern Hawk Owl*. Natural Superior, Duluth, MN.

Brinker, David F. and Katharine E. Duffy, David M. Whalen, Bryan D. Watts, and Kevin M. Dodge. 1997. *Autumn Migration of Northern Saw-whet Owls (Aegolius acadicus) in the Middle Atlantic and Northeastern United States: What Observations from 1995 Suggest*. In Duncan, Johnson, and Nicholls. 1997.

Bull, E. L. and J. R. Duncan. 1993. *Great Gray Owl (Strix nebulosa)* In *The Birds of North America*, No. 41 (A. Poole and F. Gill, eds.). The Academy of Natural Sciences. Philadelphia, PA. The American Ornithologists' Union. Washington, D.C.

Burton, John Andrew. 1984. *Owls of the World*—New Ed. Eurobook. Glasgow.

Cannings, R. J. 1993. *Northern Saw-whet Owl (Aegolius acadicus)*. In *The Birds of North America*, No. 42 (A. Poole and F. Gill, eds.). The Academy of Natural Sciences. Philadelphia, PA. The American Ornithologists' Union. Washington, D.C.

Cheveau, M. P., P. Drapeau, L. Imbeau, and Y. Bergeron. 2004. *Owl Winter Irruptions as an Indicator of Small Mammal Population Cycles in the Boreal Forest of Eastern North America*. Oikos 107:190-198.

Duncan, James R., David H. Johnson, and Thomas H. Nicholls. 1997. *Biology and Conservation of Owls in the Northern Hemisphere: Symposium Proceedings*. USDA Forest Service General Technical Report NC-190.

Duncan, James R. and Patricia A. Duncan. 1998. *Northern Hawk-Owl (Surnia ulula)*. In *The Birds of North America*, No. 356 (A. Poole and F. Gill, eds.). The Birds of North America, Inc., Philadelphia, PA.

Duncan, James. 2003. *Owls of the World*. Key Porter Books. Toronto, ON, Canada.

Dunne, Pete. 2006. *Pete Dunne's Essential Field Guide Companion*. Houghton Mifflin. New York, NY.

Eckert, Kim. 2002. *A Birder's Guide to Minnesota* (4th ed.). Gavian Guides. Duluth, MN.

Eckert, Kim. 1992. *A Record Invasion of Northern Owls*. The Loon. 64:189-195.

Eckert, Kim. 2005. *The Winter 2004-2005 Influx of Northern Owls: An Overview*. The Loon. 77:123-131.

Ehrlich, Paul R., David S. Dobkin, and Darryl Wheye. 1988. *The Birder's Handbook: A Field Guide to the Natural

Bibliography

History of North American Birds. Simon and Schuster. New York, NY.

Evans, David L. and Robert N. Rosenfield. 1987. *Remigial Molt in Fall Migrant Long-eared and Northern Saw-whet Owls*. in Nero, R. W., R.J. Clark, R. J. Knapton, and R. H. Hamre. *Biology and Conservation of Northeast Forest Owls: Symposium Proceedings*. USDA Forest Service General Technical Report RM-142.

Everett, Michael. 1977. *A Natural History of Owls*. Hamlyn. London, UK.

Gelbach, F. R. 1995 *Eastern Screech-Owl (Otus asio)*. In *The Birds of North American*, No. 165 (A. Poole and F. Gill, eds.). The Academy of Natural Sciences. Philadelphia, PA. The American Ornithologists' Union. Washington, D.C.

Godfrey, W. Earl. 1986. *The Birds of Canada* (revised). National Museum of Canada. Ottawa, ON, Canada.

Grosshuesch, David. 2003. *Observations of Nesting Northern Hawk-Owls in Minnesota*. The Loon. 75:8-14.

Haug, E. A., B. A. Millsap, and M.S. Martell. 1993. *Burrowing Owl (Athene cunicularia)*. In *The Birds of North America*, No. 61 (A. Poole and F. Gill, eds.). The Academy of Natural Sciences. Philadelphia, PA. The American Ornithologists' Union. Washington, D.C.

Hayward, G. D. and P. H. Hayward. 1993. *Boreal Owl (Aegolius funereus)*. In *The Birds of North America* (A. Poole and F. Gill, Eds.). The Birds of North America, Inc. Philadelphia, PA.

Houston, C.S., D.G. Smith, and C. Rohner. 1998. *Great Horned Owl (Bubo virginianus)*. In *The Birds of North America*, No. 372 (A. Poole and F. Gill, eds.). The Birds of North America, Inc. Philadelphia, PA.

Johnsgard, Paul A. 1988. *North American Owls: Biology and Natural History*. Smithsonian Institution Press. Washington D.C. and New York, NY.

Jonsson, Lars. 1992. *Birds of Europe with North Africa and the Middle East*. Princeton University Press. Princeton, NJ.

Kaufman, Kenn. 1996. *Lives of North American Birds*. Houghton Mifflin. Boston, MA and New York, NY.

Konig, Claus, Friedhelm Weick, and Jan-Henrik Becking. 1999. *Owls: A Guide to the Owls of the World*. Yale University Press. New Haven, CT.

Kroodsma, Donald. 2005. *The Singing Life of Birds: The Art and Science of Listening to Birdsong*. Houghton Mifflin. New York, NY.

Lane, William H., David E. Andersen, and Thomas H. Nicholls. 1997. *Habitat Use and Movements of Breeding Male Boreal Owls (Aegolius funereus) in Northeast Minnesota as Determined by Radio Telemetry,* in Duncan, James R., David H. Johnson, and Thomas H. Nicholls. 1997. *Biology and Conservation of Owls in the Northern*

Bibliography

Hemisphere: Symposium Proceedings. USDA Forest Service General Technical Report NC-190.

Marks, J.S., D.L. Evans, and D. W. Holt. 1994. *Long-eared Owl. (Asio Otus)*. In *The Birds of North America*, No. 133 (A. Poole and F. Gill, eds.). The Academy of Natural Sciences. Philadelphia, PA. The American Ornithologists' Union. Washington, D.C.

Marti, C.D. 1974. *Feeding Ecology of Four Sympatric Owls*. Condor 76:45-61.

Marti, C. D., A. F. Poole, and L. R. Bevier. 2005. *Barn Owl (Tyto alba)*. In *The Birds of North America*, No. 1 (A. Poole and F. Gill, eds.). The Birds of North America, Inc. Philadelphia, PA.

Mazur, K. M. and P.C. James. 2000. *Barred Owl (Strix varia)*. In *The Birds of North America*, No. 508 (A. Poole and F. Gill, eds.). The Birds of North America, Inc. Philadelphia, PA.

Nero, R. W. 1980. *The Great Gray Owl: Phantom of the Northern Forest*. Smithsonian Institution Press. Washington, D.C.

Nero, R. W., R.J. Clark, R. J. Knapton, and R. H. Hamre. *Biology and Conservation of Northeast Forest Owls: Symposium Proceedings*. USDA Forest Service General Technical Report RM-142.

Parmelee, David. 1992. *Snowy Owl (Nyctea scandiaca)*. In *The Birds of North America*, No. 10 (A. Poole, P.

Stettenheim, and F. Gill, eds.). The Academy of Natural Sciences. Philadelphia, PA. The American Ornithologists' Union. Washington, D.C.

Pittaway, Ron and Jean Iron. *Ageing and Variation of Great Gray Owls*. Ontario Birds. 23:138-146.

Roberts, T. S. 1932. *The Birds of Minnesota*. University of Minnesota Press, Minneapolis, MN.

Sibley, David Allen. 2001. *The Sibley Guide to Bird Life and Behavior*. Knopf. New York, NY.

Sparks, John and Tony Soper. 1989. *Owls: Their Natural and Unnatural History*. Facts on File, New York, NY.

Staav, Roland, and Thord Fransson. 1987. *Nordens Fåglar*. Norstedts. Stockholm, Sweden.

Sutton, Clay and Patricia Sutton. 1994. *How to Spot an Owl*. Chapters. Shelburne, VT.

Svingen, Peder and Frank J. Nicoletti. 2005. *The Winter Influx of Northern Owls: Part I: Northern Hawk-Owl*. The Loon. 77:132-139.

Svingen, Peder H. and James. W. Lind. 2005. *The 2004-2005 Influx of Northern Owls, Part II: Great Gray Owl*. The Loon. 77:194-208.

Svingen, Peder. 1997. *The 1996-1997 Influx of Northern Owls into Minnesota*. The Loon. 69:114-124.

Taylor, Robert R. 1997. *The Great Gray Owl: On Silent*

Further Reading

Wings. Windermere House. Winnipeg, MB, Canada.

Voronetsky, Vladimir I. 1997. *Some Features of Long-eared Owl Ecology and Behavior: Mechanisms Maintaining Territoriality*. in Duncan, James R., David H. Johnson, and Thomas H. Nicholls. 1997. *Biology and Conservation of Owls in the Northern Hemisphere: Symposium Proceedings*. USDA Forest Service General Technical Report NC-190.

Voous, Karel H. 1988. *Owls of the Northern Hemisphere*. MIT Press. Cambridge, MA.

Wiggins, D. A. 2006. *Short-eared Owl (Asio flammeus)*. In *The Birds of North America Online* (A. Poole, Ed.) Ithaca: Cornell Laboratory of Ornithology; Retrieved from the Birds of North America Online Database.

Welty, Joel Carl. 1979. *The Life of Birds*. Saunders College Publishing. Philadelphia, PA.

Wilson, Steve. 1993. *Nesting Northern Hawk-Owls*. The Loon. 65:58-60.

Yolen, Jane. 1987. *Owl Moon*. Philomel Books. New York, NY.

Duncan, James. 2003 *Owls of the World*. Key Porter Books. Toronto, ON, Canada.

Ehrlich, Paul R., David S. Dobkin, and Darryl Wheye. 1988. *The Birder's Handbook: A Field Guide to the Natural History of North American Birds*. Simon and Schuster. New York, NY.

Kaufman, Kenn. 1996. *Lives of North American Birds*. Houghton Mifflin. Boston and New York, NY.

National Geographic Society, *Birds of North America* (4th ed.) National Geographic Society, Washington, D.C.

Nero, R. W. 1980. *The Great Gray Owl: Phantom of the Northern Forest*. Smithsonian Institution Press. Washington, D.C.

Sibley, David Allen. 2001. *The Sibley Guide to Bird Life and Behavior*. Knopf. New York, NY.

Sutton, Clay and Patricia Sutton. 1994. *How to Spot an Owl*. Chapters. Shelburne, VT.

Taylor, Robert R. 1997. *The Great Gray Owl: On Silent Wings*. Windermere House. Winnipeg, MB, Canada.

Yolen, Jane. 1987. *Owl Moon*. Philomel Books. New York, NY.

Photo Credits

If we added up all the hours in the field it took to get the photos in this book, the number would be nearly unbelievable. Not to mention the conditions these photographers endured—cramped blinds, soggy feet, blood-thirsty mosquitoes, finger-numbing cold. But the results are spectacular! We collected the best of the best and searched far and wide to find them—Wyoming, Ohio, New York, Minnesota and even Finland. Hats off to all of our photographers!

Christian Artuso (www.birds-of-the-world.0catch.com) 17 (right), 25, 59, 74, 76, 77, 78 (both), 79 (all).
Ron Austing (www.ronausting.com) 64.
David Evans 67 (right).
Michael Furtman (www.michaelfurtman.com) 31 (both), 44, 56, 58 (main), 60 (left), 63.
Ron Green (www.greensphotoimages.com) 8, 26 (both), 32 (right).
Dave Grosshuesch 17 (left), 61 (bottom left).
Henry H. Holdsworth (www.wildbynaturegallery.com) 41 (right), 66.
Wilson Hum (www.pbase.com/golfpic) 23.
Tomi Muukkonen (www.birdphoto.fi) 16, 19.
Earl Orf (www.earlorfphotos.com) 28, 62, 67 (left).
Jari Peltomaki (www.birdphoto.fi) 12, 13, 38 (both), 39 (left), 40 (left), 45 (bottom right), 72 (both), 73.
Kim Risen (www.naturescapenews.com) 5, 32 (left).
Sparky Stensaas (www.sparkyphotos.com) 3, 11, 20, 22, 24, 27, 34, 35, 36, 37, 41, 42 (both), 43 (all), 45, (left, top right), 47, 48, 52, 54 (right), 55 (all), 60 (right), 61 (bottom right), 65, 68, 69, 71.
Paul Sundberg 57, 58 (inset).
Stan Tekeila (www.naturesmart.com) 39 (right top, middle and bottom).
Markus Varesvuo (www.birdphoto.fi) 9, 10, 14, 18, 50, 53, 54 (left), 61 (top), 70.
Gerrit Vyn (www.gerritvynphoto.com) 33 (left).
Yellowstone National Park 33 (right).
Jim Zipp (www.jimzipp.com) 21, 30, 46, 75.

Index

Index